THE
Center Stage
JOURNAL

For Moms Ready to Choose
Themselves

Satya V. Nauth

Praise for The Center Stage Journal

"The Center Stage Journal felt like it was written for the moment motherhood shifts and you're left asking, 'Who am I now?' As an empty-nester, the prompts helped me process years of self-sacrifice while gently guiding me back to my own voice, confidence, and desires. It honors the depth of motherhood while making room for what comes next—reminding mothers that they still belong at the center of their own story" — Diane Jagessar, host of Beyond the Sugarcoat.

"As a woman building my life and dreaming of becoming a wife and mother, The Center Stage Journal felt both affirming and timely. It reframes motherhood not as a season of self-loss, but as one of presence, confidence, and intentional living. The prompts encouraged me to release guilt, trust my voice, and honor myself while loving others. This journal is a reminder that showing up fully for future family begins with claiming my place at the center of my own story today"— T.D. Balram, Founder of Enlighten Education.

Praise for Satya's Book, Mom Take Center Stage

"Engaging and insightful, Mom Take Center Stage provides affirming, enduring advice on motherhood and self-love." — BookLife by Publishers Weekly

This journal is most powerful when used alongside:

MOM TAKE CENTER STAGE

Unfiltered. Unapologetic. Unstoppable. A Guide for Moms Ready to Reclaim the Spotlight

Scan to learn more:

Take Center Stage with Me

Before you dive in, I want to invite you to stay connected beyond these pages.

Visit SatyaNauth.com (https://satyanauth.com) to access free resources, behind-the-scenes insights, and weekly encouragement created just for moms like you—those ready to live boldly and lead from within.

Email: MomTakeCenterStage@gmail.com

➡️📱 Scan the QR code to connect instantly and to begin your journey now.

This journal belongs to:

_____

_____

May these pages bring your truth to light.

Inside This Journal

This journal is not meant to be completed in order. Begin wherever you feel called.

Welcome to *The Center Stage Journal*

This is your canvas — your space, your pause, your exhale, your reminder that you are more than the roles you juggle and the expectations you carry.

If you're here feeling uncertain, stretched thin, or quietly questioning yourself — you're not behind. You're human. This journal was created for the moments when confidence wavers, self-doubt creeps in, and mom guilt makes you second-guess your needs, your choices, or your worth.

Here, in these pages, you get to choose yourself because you have waited long enough.

And the time isn't someday.
It's not when life slows down.
It's not after everyone else is settled.

It's Now.

This journal is your personal manifesto — a place to build confidence, release guilt, quiet the inner critic, and reconnect with the woman beneath the noise. Inside, you'll meet prompts that challenge you, pages that free you, and reflections that remind you of your strength — even on the days you forget it.

You won't be asked to be perfect. Come exactly as you are—willing, learning, and growing. Bring honesty. Bring patience for yourself. You will only be asked to show up as yourself — curious, open, and willing to step into the power you were born to claim.

Every page is a step toward the version of you who trusts her voice, honors her needs, protects her peace, and leads her life with intention. The woman who doesn't shrink. The woman who doesn't apologize for existing. The woman who knows she belongs at the center of her own story.

Take your time here.
Scribble. Explore. Release. Celebrate.
This journal isn't a test — it's a *becoming*.

You *are* the main character of your story.
You can be fully you— whole.
You *will* take center stage.

Let's begin.

Building Confidence

Confidence isn't about being perfect nor is it just self-assurance. It's about showing up fully in your knowingness. It's knowing your voice matters, your choices matter, and yes—you can develop the ability to trust firmly in yourself. You can and will own your confidence.

Quick-Punch

Write about 3 things you did last week that made you proud. Don't be humble. Celebrate loud.

1.

_____

_____

_____

_____

_____

2.

_____

_____

_____

_____

_____

3.

_____

_____

_____

_____

_____

_____

Take Action

What's one small risk you can take this week to stretch your confidence? Write it down. Then do it.

_____

_____

_____

_____

_____

_____

Bold Reminder

Repeat and Practice:

I SHOW UP. I SPEAK. I MATTER. I AM SEEN.

How did this bold reminder make you feel?

_____

_____

_____

_____

_____

_____

_____

_____

_____

Reflect

Think of a time you doubted yourself. Now write what you'd tell that version of you today.

_____

_____

_____

_____

_____

_____

_____

_____

Off My Chest

This is your space to let it all out — the thoughts that loop in your head, the feelings you swallow, the frustrations you pretend do not bother you. No filters. No fixing. Just truth on paper. Write until you feel lighter. This is where release begins and clarity follows.

_____

_____

_____

_____

_____

_____

_____

_____

_____

_____

_____

Confidence in Daily Life

Where can you flex confidence this week? At home? At work? With friends? Be specific.

_____

_____

_____

_____

_____

_____

_____

_____

_____

Micro-Challenge

Say YES to one thing that stretches you this week. Then write how it felt.

_____

_____

_____

_____

_____

_____

_____

_____

_____

_____

Spot the Sabotage

Where do you hold yourself back? Why? Write it out. Decide what ends here. Not next week. Not when you feel ready. Begin where you are.

_____

_____

_____

_____

_____

_____

_____

_____

_____

Bold Affirmation

I TRUST MY VOICE. I TRUST MY DECISIONS. I TRUST ME.

Confidence at Home

How can you show up more fully with your kids or partner this week?
Pour out one action step.

_____

_____

_____

_____

_____

_____

_____

_____

_____

Confidence at Work/Business

Where can you speak up, take the lead, or assert yourself at work or in your business? Name it.

_____

_____

_____

_____

_____

_____

_____

_____

_____

_____

Off My Chest (Unfiltered)

This is your rebel space. No rules, no edits, no apologies. Say it. Spill it. Write it.

_____

_____

_____

_____

_____

_____

_____

_____

_____

Offload and Own It

Who can you hand responsibility to this week so you can show up stronger? Kids, partner, team—name them and write it down.

_____

_____

_____

_____

_____

_____

_____

_____

_____

_____

Brag a Little

List 5 things you've done this month that showed courage, strength, or confidence. Be proud.

1.

_____

_____

_____

_____

_____

2.

_____

_____

_____

_____

_____

3.

_____

_____

_____

_____

_____

4.

_____

_____

_____

_____

_____

5.

_____

_____

_____

_____

_____

Face It, Name It, Release It

Notice the fear, doubt, shame, or frustration lurking inside. Name it. Call it out. Put it on the page. Then let it go. This is your safe space to drop the weight you've been carrying and reclaim your energy. No edits. No judgment. Just release.

_____

_____

_____

_____

_____

_____

_____

_____

_____

_____

Mirror Room Visual

Step into the mirror — the space where you meet the truest version of yourself. This is you—*fully confident, unstoppable, unapologetic.* Write what she looks like, how she moves, what she says, and how she owns every room she enters.

_____

_____

_____

_____

_____

_____

_____

_____

_____

Power Move

Pick one fearless move you will make this week. Write it like a contract with yourself—commit, promise, OWN it. This is non-negotiable. You show up. You step into your power. You do this.

I, _____, promise to speak up in every meeting this week. I will own my ideas, trust my voice, and refuse to shrink. I commit to taking action even when it scares me. This is my non-negotiable commitment to myself.

_____

_____

_____

_____

_____

_____

_____

_____

_____

Wild Pages

This is your untamed space. No rules, no structure, no judgment. Sketch. Scribble. Write gratitude lists. Brainstorm. Rant. Dream. Spill ideas. Anything goes. These pages are yours—raw, free, and completely wild.

_____

_____

_____

_____

_____

_____

_____

_____

_____

_____

_____

_____

_____

_____

_____

_____

_____

_____

_____

_____

Let Yourself Off the Hook

You've apologized for things that didn't deserve an apology. You've felt guilty for taking breaks, for saying no, for craving your own pursuits, for not doing more — even when you were doing everything.

But guilt isn't proof of love. It's just evidence of excessive pressure — the invisible kind that tells moms they have to earn their worth through self-sacrifice. You've done enough. You are enough. It's time to let yourself off the hook.

Face It, Name It, Release It

What occurrences trigger your guilt most often? (Be honest — even the small, everyday ones.)

_____

_____

_____

_____

_____

_____

Who benefits when you stay trapped in guilt? Who loses when you stay small?

_____

_____

_____

_____

_____

_____

What would it feel like to trade guilt for grace?

_____

_____

_____

_____

_____

Write a new story for motherhood — one that gives you room to breathe, grow, and be human.

_____

_____

_____

_____

_____

Self-Reflection: The Double Standard

We often expect perfection from ourselves but give grace to everyone else.

Reflect on a time when your child or partner made a mistake.

What did you tell them? (*"It's okay," "You did your best," "Try again."*)

Now — adopt the same script. Tell yourself those same words.

Write them down here, exactly as you would say them to someone you love.

_____

_____

_____

_____

_____

_____

_____

_____

Forgive Yourself

Forgiveness isn't weakness — it's *self-liberation.*
Finish these lines and let them land.

I forgive myself for believing I had to be perfect to be loved.

_____

_____

_____

I forgive myself for the moments I lost my patience or doubted my strength.

_____

_____

_____

I forgive myself for forgetting who I am outside of being a mom.

_____

_____

_____

I now choose to honor myself by…

_____

_____

_____

Off My Chest

Let it out.

What's one story or untruth you've been telling yourself that keeps you stuck in guilt?

Maybe it's the belief that "I'm selfish for enjoying time away from my kids" or "I'm a bad mom for getting angry."

Write it here — then rewrite it with compassion.

_____

_____

_____

_____

_____

_____

_____

_____

Wild Pages

Use these lines to reclaim your joy.

List everything that brings you peace — no guilt, no explanation.

Write about moments that remind you of who you were before the world told you to prove yourself.

Draw, dream, plan — this is where freedom begins.

_____

_____

_____

_____

_____

_____

_____

_____

_____

_____

_____

_____

_____

_____

_____

_____

_____

_____

_____

_____

_____

_____

_____

_____

Bold You

What does guilt-free you look like?

How does she walk, speak, parent, and live?

What's one decision she would make today to honor her own peace?

Write it like a declaration of freedom.

_____

_____

_____

_____

_____

_____

_____

_____

_____

_____

_____

Affirmation

I'M NOT HERE TO PERFORM WORTHINESS. WORTHINESS ISN'T A FALLACY — I ALREADY HAVE IT. I CHOOSE PEACE OVER PERFECTION. I RELEASE GUILT, EMBRACE GRACE, AND LET MYSELF OFF THE HOOK.

Both/And

You can't pour from an empty cup, but you also can't fill it if guilt keeps poking holes in the bottom. Mom guilt thrives on the lie that love equals self-sacrifice — that your worth is measured by how much you give, not how worthy you are.

It's time to rewrite that story. You can be a devoted mom and a fulfilled woman. You can be soft and powerful. You can love your family and fight for your dreams. You're allowed both.

Face It, Name It, Release It

Where in your life do you feel like you're constantly choosing between two parts of yourself? Spot and note the duality.

_____

_____

_____

What's one way you've dulled your light to set someone else at ease?

_____

_____

_____

How would your life look if you stopped picking parts of you and started integrating all of you?

_____

_____

_____

Write a declaration that starts with:

I can be both _____ and

_____.

Off My Chest

Write about a moment when you felt guilty for choosing yourself — saying no, setting a boundary, pursuing a dream or maybe taking time for yourself.

Now, look at that moment again through the lens of your worth.

Did you really do something *wrong* — or something *right* for your wellbeing?

_____

_____

_____

_____

_____

_____

_____

_____

_____

Wild Pages

Use this space to vent, reflect, or celebrate moments where you chose you. Draw, list, or write about the things that make you feel alive beyond motherhood. This is your permission slip — to be whole, to be human, and to stop apologizing for it.

_____

_____

_____

_____

_____

_____

_____

_____

_____

_____

_____

_____

_____

_____

_____

_____

_____

_____

_____

_____

_____

_____

_____

Self-Trust: Whole Without Approval

Your worth isn't measured by anyone else's validation. You're already worthy. You are enough. This section is about trusting your voice, honoring your instincts, and claiming your life unapologetically. Own your decisions. Celebrate your intuition. Write it down. Let it stick.

Reflect

Think of a recent choice you second-guessed. How did it make you feel? How would it feel if you fully trusted your decision? Don't hold back. Share all of your thoughts and feelings.

_____

_____

_____

_____

_____

_____

_____

_____

_____

_____

_____

Micro-Challenge

This week, make one decision without seeking approval or advice. Write down what it is and how it feels to trust yourself fully. Track your emotions afterward.

_____

_____

_____

_____

_____

_____

_____

_____

_____

Past Wins

Recall 3 moments in your life when trusting yourself paid off. Write them down and feel the power of your own voice.

1.

_____

_____

_____

2.

_____

_____

_____

3.

_____

_____

_____

Letter of Forgiveness

Forgive yourself for the times you ignored your voice. Write a letter of forgiveness to yourself and release it here. Use the example below or write your own.

Dear Me,

I forgive you for the times you doubted yourself. For every "yes" you gave when your gut said "no." For every moment you let someone else's opinion decide your worth. I forgive you for shrinking, over-giving, and ignoring your own voice.

From this day forward, I promise to listen to you first, trust your instincts, and honor your needs without guilt. You are enough. You always were. You always will be.

With love and fierce respect,
Me

_____

_____

_____

_____

_____

_____

Power Reminder

I honor my choices. I trust my instincts. I am whole without anyone's approval.

_____

_____

_____

_____

_____

_____

_____

_____

_____

Self-Pledge

I, _____, commit to trusting my voice, honoring my instincts, and believing in my worth without needing approval. I will listen to myself first and show up for me. This is my non-negotiable pledge.

_____

_____

_____

_____

_____

_____

_____

_____

_____

Signature_____

Date_____

Wild Pages

Overflow thoughts, gratitude, ideas, or reflections on self-trust. Let it flow. No judgment. Wild Pages are yours.

_____

_____

_____

_____

_____

_____

_____

_____

_____

_____

_____

_____

_____

_____

_____

_____

_____

_____

_____

_____

_____

_____

_____

_____

Boundaries: Protecting Your Peace and What You've Built

Having boundaries doesn't mean that you have erected walls barring others from you. Instead, they're doors that lead back to yourself. They keep your energy pure, your peace intact, and your priorities honed. When you set one, you're not saying no to others—you're saying "yes" to the you, you're becoming.

Quick Punch

Where in your life are you saying "yes" while your inner voice is whispering "no"?

_____

_____

_____

_____

_____

_____

_____

_____

_____

_____

Reflection

Which relationship, commitment, or habit drains you most right now? What feels possible if you stopped over-explaining and started honoring yourself?

_____

_____

_____

_____

_____

_____

_____

_____

_____

Off My Chest

What's something you've been carrying silently because you didn't want to disappoint someone? Say it here—without softening, fixing, or justifying it.

_____

_____

_____

_____

_____

_____

_____

_____

_____

_____

Boundary in Practice (Micro Challenge)

This week, pause before saying "yes." Ask yourself a pivotal question, *"Do I actually have the capacity for this?"* If not, practice responding in a way that protects your peace.

What does that sound like for *you?*

_____

_____

_____

_____

_____

_____

_____

_____

_____

_____

Past Wins

Recall a time when setting a boundary actually improved your life or solidified a relationship. What did this experience teach you?

_____

_____

_____

_____

_____

_____

_____

_____

_____

_____

Release

Where are you still overextending in hopes of approval or validation? What would be the outcome if you stopped negotiating your worth?

_____

_____

_____

_____

_____

_____

_____

_____

_____

Forgiveness

Who do you need to forgive—yourself or someone else—for crossing, abandoning or ignoring a boundary? Write a note of release. This is for you.

_____

_____

_____

_____

_____

_____

_____

_____

_____

_____

Power Reminder

Establishing boundaries don't make you difficult—they make you dependable to the person you depend on most: *yourself.* You can't pour from a cracked cup.

_____

_____

_____

_____

_____

_____

_____

_____

_____

_____

Wild Pages

No structure. No rules.

Sketch, vent, list, or write anything that helps you reclaim your energy and come back to yourself.

_____

_____

_____

_____

_____

_____

_____

_____

_____

_____

_____

_____

_____

_____

_____

_____

_____

_____

_____

_____

_____

_____

_____

_____

_____

Taking Center Stage

You've done the work—building confidence, setting boundaries, trusting yourself. Now, it's time to step forward.

Taking center stage isn't about ego. It's about ownership. Your presence matters. Your voice shapes your legacy. The world doesn't need a quieter version of you—it needs the whole, unfiltered truth of who you are.

Quick-Punch

What does 'taking center stage' mean to you right now? What would it look like, sound like, or feel like in your life?

_____

_____

_____

_____

_____

_____

_____

_____

_____

Power Reminder

I AM NOT HIDING. I AM SHOWING UP—
FULLY, FIERCELY, AND FREE.

Reflect

Think about the women who've inspired you. What qualities did they own that you're ready to embrace too?

_____

_____

_____

_____

_____

_____

_____

_____

_____

Off My Chest

What fears still hold you back from taking your stage? Fear of judgment? Rejection? Failure, or being "too much"? Name it here—and take its power away.

_____

_____

_____

_____

_____

_____

_____

_____

_____

_____

Micro-Challenge

This week, do one thing that makes you visible—post your work, speak up, wear the outfit, ask for what you want. Write it down and commit. What will you do?

_____

_____

_____

_____

_____

_____

_____

_____

_____

Pass the Baton

What responsibilities or mental loads are keeping you backstage? Who can you delegate to so that you can focus on what lights you up?

_____

_____

_____

_____

_____

_____

_____

_____

_____

Leave Your Mark

What values do you want your kids—or anyone watching you—to see in the way you live?

List your top 3 legacy values.

1.

_____

_____

_____

2.

_____

_____

_____

3.

_____

_____

_____

_____

Release

Let go of any guilt around wanting more, shining brighter, or outgrowing old versions of yourself. Write it down and let it go.

_____

_____

_____

_____

_____

_____

_____

_____

_____

_____

Legacy in Action

What's one small action you can take this week that reflects the legacy you want to leave? A conversation. A boundary. A creative step. Write it here and follow through.

_____

_____

_____

_____

_____

_____

_____

_____

_____

Proof of Growth

What's one moment you're proud of that shows how far you've already come? This is evidence. Write it down.

_____

_____

_____

_____

_____

_____

_____

_____

_____

Power Reminder

I AM THE AUTHOR OF MY STORY, THE DIRECTOR OF MY DAYS, AND THE LEADING WOMAN OF MY LIFE.

Future Vision

Imagine yourself five years from now—grounded, confident, and fully in your worth. How does she move? What's different? What feels easier? What has she stopped apologizing for?

_____

_____

_____

_____

_____

_____

_____

_____

_____

_____

Legacy Pledge

I,_____, commit to taking center stage in my life. I will no longer dim my light, silence my truth, or wait for permission. I choose to live with purpose, confidence, worth and unapologetic joy.

My legacy starts now.

_____

_____

_____

_____

_____

_____

_____

_____

_____

Signature_____

Date_____

Legacy Note to Self

Dear Me,

You've carried so much, loved deeply, and worked tirelessly for everyone else. But now, it's your turn. You deserve to be seen, celebrated, and remembered for who you truly are—not just what you do for others.

Keep showing up. Keep trusting your light. This is your center stage, and you belong here.

With gratitude and power,
Me

Now write your own "Legacy Note to Self." Start it however you wish—Dear Me, Dear [Your Name], or Dear Future Self—and let it flow.

_____

_____

_____

_____

_____

_____

_____

Wild Pages

Your stage. Your story.

Use these pages for overflow thoughts, gratitude, sketches or reflections on the legacy you're creating. Write freely.

_____

_____

_____

_____

_____

_____

_____

_____

_____

_____

_____

_____

_____

_____

_____

_____

_____

_____

_____

_____

_____

_____

Unbound

You can't take center stage if your past still has you bound backstage. This section is about release — not rewriting history, but reclaiming your story. You've carried enough. Now, you get to decide what stays and what goes.

Face It, Name It, Release It

I will not internalize the mean things people have done to me. Instead, I will…

_____

_____

_____

_____

_____

_____

_____

_____

_____

Bold Affirmation

I REALIZE IF I ALLOW PAST HURTS TO ECHO IN MY LIFE RIGHT NOW, THEN I'M EMPOWERING THOSE HURTS TO CONTINUE HURTING ME.

Off My Chest

Write about a moment from your past that still lingers. What would you say to that version of yourself — the one who was trying her best with what she knew then?

Let it all spill out here. No filters. No editing. Just truth.

_____

_____

_____

_____

_____

_____

_____

_____

_____

_____

_____

Forgive, and Be Free

Sometimes we need to forgive ourselves, too — for what we tolerated, for what we didn't know, for the ways we showed up in survival mode instead of strength.

Write a note of forgiveness to yourself here. Let it be raw and real. You're not excusing the past —you're reclaiming peace.

I forgive myself for…

_____

_____

_____

_____

_____

_____

_____

_____

I now choose to move forward by…

_____

_____

_____

_____

_____

_____

_____

_____

_____

_____

Release Old Stories

What's one hurt or betrayal you've been carrying that you're finally ready to release? Write about it here. This is your clean slate.

_____

_____

_____

_____

_____

_____

_____

_____

_____

_____

Past Lessons and Growth

I may have faced tragedies and set backs, but they don't define me. The struggles have forged my awakening. Good things came from those situations:

1.

_____

_____

_____

_____

2.

_____

_____

_____

_____

3.

_____

_____

_____

_____

_____

4.

_____

_____

_____

_____

_____

I wear my pain like armor, and I do so by…

_____

_____

_____

_____

_____

_____

_____

_____

_____

Wild Pages

Use these pages however you need.

Scribble the words you never got to say.

Sketch what forgiveness feels like.

List what you're done apologizing for.

This is your release ritual — raw, real, and yours.

_____

_____

_____

_____

_____

_____

_____

_____

_____

_____

_____

_____

_____

_____

_____

_____

_____

_____

_____

_____

_____

_____

_____

_____

_____

_____

_____

_____

_____

_____

_____

_____

_____

Fiercely Unbound

What's one way you'll show up differently now that you're unbound? Write it like a promise to yourself — loud, proud, and definitive.

_____

_____

_____

_____

_____

_____

_____

_____

_____

Power Reminder

I AM NO LONGER CARRYING THE LIFE EXPERIENCES OR THE PEOPLE THAT BROKE ME.

I AM BUILDING FROM IT — FREE, WHOLE, AND UNBOUND.

The Center Stage Manifesto

This is your final act in the journal—a space and moment to integrate everything you've discovered and declare who you are, unapologetically. Your manifesto is your commitment to yourself: how you will show up, honor your worth, and live boldly. This is your declaration that you belong at the center of your own story.

Celebrate Your Wins

Reflect on your journey through this journal. What shifts have you noticed in yourself?

List 5 ways you've grown through this process:

1.

_____

_____

2.

_____

_____

3.

_____

_____

4.

_____

_____

5.

_____

_____

Lessons Learned

What key lessons about yourself, your worth, and your power do you want to carry forward?

Write 3-5 lessons that have changed the way you see yourself:

1.

_____

_____

2.

_____

_____

3.

_____

_____

4.

_____

_____

5.

_____

_____

My Daily/Weekly Rituals

How will you maintain this growth in your daily life?

Write 3-5 practices, habits, or rituals that will keep you centered and aligned with your power:

1.

_____

_____

2.

_____

_____

3.

_____

_____

4.

_____

_____

5.

_____

_____

My Personal Power Statement

Create a declaration that captures your unapologetic self, your boundaries, and your voice. Make it bold, present tense, and yours.

I am

_____

_____

_____

I show up

_____

_____

_____

I claim

_____

_____

_____

My Legacy Promise

Reflect on the lasting impact you want to leave in your family, friendships, work or community. This is your commitment to living fully and authentically.

I will leave a legacy of

_____

_____

_____

I will live in alignment with

_____

_____

_____

I will model

_____

_____

_____

Center Stage Manifesto

This is your declaration. Your bold statement of self. A reminder that every page you've written, every truth you've faced, every fear you've released has led you here. Read it aloud. Own it. Let it guide you as you move forward.

I, _____,
commit to stepping into my life fully. I will no longer dim my light, silence my voice, or shrink to make others comfortable.

I will celebrate my wins and embrace my lessons.

I will honor my boundaries, trust my instincts, and nurture my confidence.

I will choose myself with courage, clarity, and grace—every day, in every way.

I will live unapologetically, fiercely, and with intention.

I am the main character of my story. I am whole. I am enough. I take center stage.

Wild Pages

Use these pages to write, sketch, or brainstorm anything else that feels important. This is your final release and creation space. Celebrate your growth and power.

_____

_____

_____

_____

_____

_____

_____

_____

_____

_____

_____

_____

_____

_____

_____

_____

_____

_____

_____

_____

_____

_____

_____

About the Author

Satya V. Nauth is the author of *Mom Take Center Stage*, a book written for women who are ready to stop shrinking and start shining.

She is an entrepreneur and personal growth advocate with a background in marketing, leadership development, and the short-term rental industry. She lives in Florida with her family, where life is full, vibrant, and always a little messy—in the best way.

When she's not writing or running her business, you'll likely find her with a book in hand or walking under the evening sky, reflecting on life's many layers. She believes in the quiet power of intentional living, the boldness of taking center stage, and the beauty of stories that give voice to the unspoken truths of modern womanhood.

Continue Taking Center Stage

This is the beginning of your bold, purpose-filled journey.

Here's how you can keep showing up for your life—and for yourself:

✦ Join the Movement

Sign up for tools, reflections, and first access to what's next.

SatyaNauth.com (https://satyanauth.com) or go there directly by scanning the QR code:

🎤 Invite Me to Speak

Want to bring the message of *Mom Take Center Stage* and *The Center Stage Journal* to your community, group, or event?

➤ SatyaNauth.com (https://satyanauth.com/contact/)

💬 Connect and Share

Follow along on:

Instagram/Tik Tok: @Satya_Nauth
Facebook: https://facebook.com/satya.nauth.3
Email: MomTakeCenterStage@gmail.com

If this journal moved something in you…

If these pages helped you see yourself differently, set a boundary you'd been avoiding, or take center stage in a new way, I'd be honored if you shared a few words about your experience.

Your reflection may be the permission another woman needs to begin.

You can share your experience wherever you purchased this journal.

Tag #MomTakeCenterStage and #TheCenterStageJournal to let the world see how you're taking the lead.

You're not just a reader—you're part of a movement. And this is your moment.

www.ingramcontent.com/pod-product-compliance
Lightning Source LLC
Chambersburg PA
CBHW020742130626
46554CB00006B/2106